Fur, Fe[athers] or Skin

Written by Jo Windsor

Some animals
have fur or wool.
Some animals
have feathers.
Some animals
have skin with
no fur or feathers.

2

This goat has wool.
It lives in the
mountains.
In the winter,
it is very cold.
The wool will keep
the goat warm.

This duck
has feathers.
The duck can use
the feathers
in its nest.
The feathers keep
the baby ducks
warm.

This bird has feathers.
It is in the long grass.
It is hiding.
The feathers help it
to hide.
The feathers help
to keep the bird safe.

These birds have
no feathers on their necks.
They have no feathers
on their head.
They like to eat animals
for their food.
When they eat food,
their heads will stay
clean.

head

neck

These animals
have no fur and
they have no feathers.
They are called mole rats.
They live under
the ground.
How do the mole rats
keep warm?

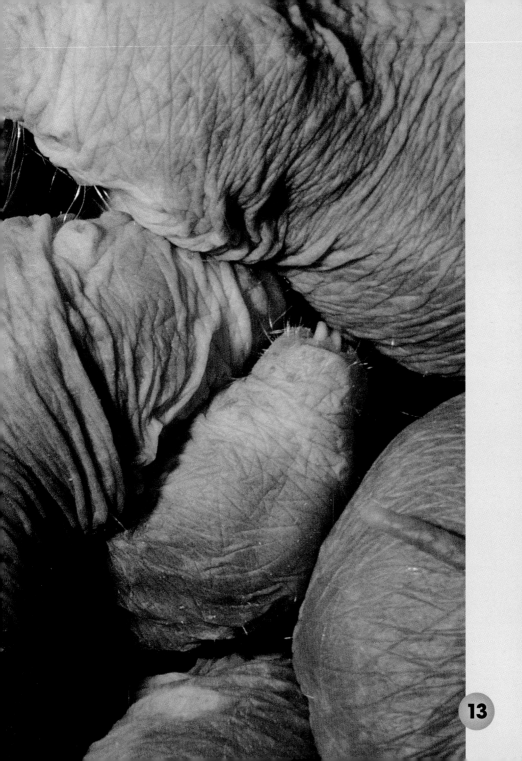

Some animals have fur or wool.
Some animals have feathers.
Some animals have skin with
no fur or feathers.

**Animals with
fur or wool**

**Animals with
feathers**

Index

**Animals with
no fur or feathers**

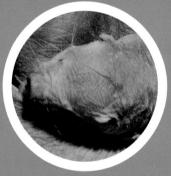

Guide Notes

> **Title: Fur, Feathers, or Skin**
> **Stage:** Early (4) – Green
>
> **Genre:** Non-fiction
> **Approach:** Guided Reading
> **Processes:** Thinking Critically, Exploring Language, Processing Information
> **Written and Visual Focus:** Photographs (static images), Labels, Index,
>   Classification Chart
> **Word Count:** 167

THINKING CRITICALLY
(sample questions)
- Look at the title and read it to the children. Ask: "What do you think this book is going to tell us?"
- Ask the children: "What animals do you know that have fur? What animals do you know that have feathers?"
- Focus the children's attention on the index. Ask: "What are you going to find out about in this book?"
- If you want to find out about animals with no fur or feathers on their heads, on which page would you look?
- If you want to find out about animals with no fur or no feathers anywhere, on which pages would you look?
- Look at page 4. What do you think might happen to the goat's coat in summer? Why?
- Look at pages 8 and 9. How do you think the feathers help to keep the bird safe?

EXPLORING LANGUAGE

Terminology
Title, cover, photographs, author, photographers

Vocabulary
Interest words: fur, wool, feathers, skin, mountains
High-frequency words: keep, called, or
Positional words: under, in, on

Print Conventions
Capital letter for sentence beginnings, full stops, commas, question mark